Debt Management For The Single Daddy

Managing Debt, Build Wealth And Live A More Fulfilling Life

Nick Thomas

Copyright © 2015 Nick Thomas

All rights reserved

No part of this book may be reproduced in any form or by any electronic or mechanical means including information storage and retrieval systems, without permission in writing from the author. The only exception is by a reviewer, who may quote short excepts in a review.

Although the author and publisher have made every effort to ensure that the information in this book was correct at press time, the author and publisher do not assume and hereby disclaim any liability to any party for any loss, damage, or disruption caused by errors or omissions, whether such errors or omissions result from negligence, accident, or any other cause.

Visit my website at www.singledaddydating.com

ISBN-13: 978-1505250787

ISBN-10: 1505250781

JOIN OUR COMMUNITY!

Single Daddy Dating is a growing community of single fathers who look to help each other, not only with dating success but in all areas of their lives too. This includes parenting, career and finances advice.

Join us today and get '**10 Crucial Checklist To Dating Success For Single Fathers**' completely FREE!

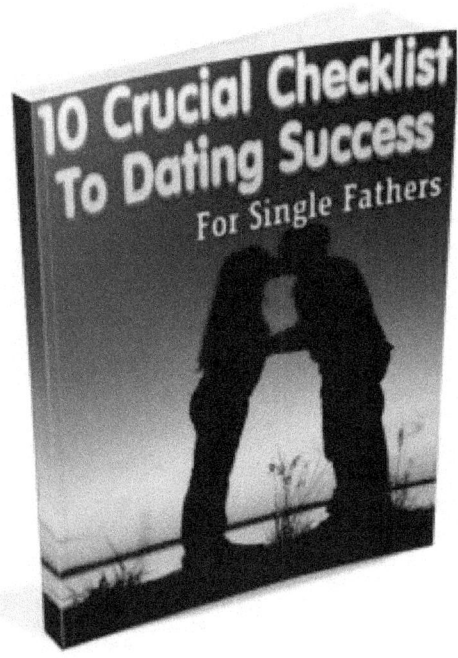

JOIN US AT
WWW.SINGLEDADDYDATING.COM/
NEWSLETTER/

DEBT MANAGEMENT

CONTENTS

Chapter 1: The Agony Of Being In Debt 1

Chapter 2: Why Are You In Debt 7

Chapter 3: The Detrimental Effects Of Being In Debt 13

Chapter 4: Priority Expenses For A Single Father 20

Chapter 5: What Are You Entitled To? 24

Chapter 6: Eliminating Debt In Your Life 29

Chapter 7: Financial Strategies For Single Fathers 37

Chapter 8: Develop A Healthy Attitude Towards Debt 42

Chapter 9: Develop An Attitude Of Prosperity 46

Final Notes 51

Chapter 1: The Agony Of Being In Debt

The first few months after a divorce can be a misery. Things seem uncertain, even if it seems like I had a new lease of life as a single father. It is like I was given a new life, but there were uncertainty in every areas of my life.

I didn't know what I was doing. I was going through the routines of going to work but I felt a lack of purpose. This feeling made me vulnerable. The only way I could forget this feeling was to indulge. I had to do something to make me forget this feeling.

What did I do?

I spent money. Lots of it, even when I was going through financial changes in my life too.

I got into debt, buying things I didn't need to try to forget the misery of divorce. Divorce has this weird way of changing you. It makes you feel like you are carefree although it seems more like you refuse to care about anything. I bought plenty of things that I didn't needed. I got myself a couple of latest mobile phones in the space of a few months, bought a slick new car and dined at places which were so expensive I never imagined myself being there before.

As a single father, or anyone for that matter, it is difficult to live happily if you have debt. I'm sorry to sound fatalistic, but it's true. I doubt you know anyone without any debt, but the truth of the matter is that many people are struggling with debt. Debt is something that binds us, like a chain on our ankles – controlling our every move and slowing us down when we think of running.

DEBT MANAGEMENT

Single fathers are the same. The reason why many single fathers are stuck in debt is due to the combination of a lack of financial management, bad habits and emotional spending. This factors causes single fathers to end up in terrible debt situations. For me, it really put me in a terrible financial position that tied me down for a couple of years.

I spent to fill a void within myself. I felt that every spending I made was to make myself feel better – so I can forget about the divorce. Over time, I had a big hole in my pockets. I was struggling to make the minimum payments on my credit cards and my interest only accrued.

I have met single fathers who resort to using their credit cards endlessly to make ends meet, after the divorce. It seems to be an easy way out – using their credit cards all the time, but they seem to have no choice because after a divorce, their expenses simply grow out of control.

After a divorce, a single father may need to pay additional alimony and child support. This is a heavy burden on his finances. Besides that, he may need to pay the mortgage which his ex-wife is now comfortably living in while he has to move out to another rented place.

This is a very common situation that single fathers need to face after a divorce. He pays for double 'rent'. Coupled with alimony and child support, he won't have much money to spare from there on. To write this book, I have asked a couple of my single fathers about their finances. Although a person's finances are a sensitive issue, these five single fathers were willing to tell me how they were doing.

From the five of them, I learned that for many single fathers, a single father only have around ten percent of his take home pay after paying for all those expenses. After deducting the mortgage on the house his ex-wife is staying, the rental of the house he is staying, alimony and child support; that was what most of them have.

This is a common situation that many single fathers are in. Imagine being in this scenario where you are left with only 10% of your take home pay each month. It is a real disaster.

No wonder so many single fathers end up in debt!

After a divorce, both the husband and wife would take a hit financially. According to statistics, single parents' debt are widespread. Among the staggering statistics include:-

- 40% of single parents are 'always in debt', while only 28% of couples are in the similar position.

- Single parents are twice as likely to have arrears on their household or consumer bills.

- Many single parents are forced to borrow from doorstep lenders

- Single parents are more likely to have longstanding debt compared to two-parent family.

These statistics can shock any single father. If you are a single father, you would be able to relate to many of these situations.

In this book, I would share strategies for you to learn how to manage your debt and slowly get out of it. If you are a single father who is looking to have more freedom and financial success, getting out of debt is a good goal to have. It would be hard to live happily if you are always worried about making payments on your debt.

From this book, you would learn about the various factors that impact your debt. It includes understanding the mindset that causes you to constantly get into debt, the detrimental effects, managing it and eliminating it.

However, getting out of debt is only a small part of the financial game. You also need to learn how to develop a healthy attitude towards money. You need to develop an attitude of abundance in all areas of your life. This would be covered in the later chapters.

Chapter 2: Why Are You In Debt

Answer this honestly: *Why are you in debt?*

What makes you get into debt? Is it something emotional?

It is very easy for people to give excuses for their debt problems. They may come out with a million excuses for their debt problems, but most of them would be blamed on external circumstances.

They would blame it on having to spend excessive amount of money on their children, alimony or mortgage. They may tell you that the cost of housing is rising endlessly. They may tell you that their bosses are to blame for not giving them a rise in salary. They may tell you that their children are to blame for demanding so much from them.

Blaming external circumstances is an easy way out. It makes you immune to criticism. It makes other people the problem and yourself the victims.

When you notice this pattern of blaming external circumstances, it may be hard for you to admit it. It is a pattern that takes away power from yourself. When you blame external circumstances, you become disempowered.

I don't mean to say that there aren't factor that contribute to your financial situation. Sure, your children, alimony, child support and mortgage plays a factor. What I'm talking about is how much power you are giving to external circumstance.

Instead, what you can do is stop blaming those circumstances and find ways to deal with the problem. You need to deal with the bad habits that put you in this terrible financial situation and seek ways to manage this situation. You need to give yourself the power to make the change, rather than constantly blame external circumstances.

For many single fathers, the real reason they get into such debt situations is because they lack the discipline to deal with the problems they have. Anyone who lack discipline in managing their money would end up in debt, not only single fathers. When you don't have the control over your finances, you would end up being deep in debt. As simple as that.

The convenience of credit is another main reason for the problem of debt. Nowadays, it seems so easy to get into debt because everyone is encouraging you to borrow money. From credit cards to college loans to the mortgage on your house, all these are baits to get you deeper into debt. I once walked into a college campus and was shocked to see how many banks offering credit card to students. Crazy, I tell you!

We live in this culture of debt and single fathers can't run away from it.

As single fathers get into these 'baits', together with their failure to plan their expenses; they only fall further into debt. Added to it is the problem of rising cost of raising a child. Unless a single father truly manages his finances strictly, things would only get worse for him.

It doesn't matter if you get sole or joint custody of the child, you still need to play an important role in managing your expenses. This part is crucial to managing debt. You need to take time to track where your money is going, whether those expenses are important and if you are paying too much of alimony.

Alimony and child support aren't final. Even if the court decides that you would need to pay $X amount each month, there is still a possibility where you can reduce your alimony payments.

You may need to communicate effectively with your ex-wife to reduce those payments. As such, managing your debt as a single father isn't only about dealing with the numbers but with the people involved as well.

These people would include your ex-wife, children and other people who would play a factor in your finances. This make debt management for single fathers a very unique challenge. It is not only about your financial expertise which would be challenged but also your emotional quotient (EQ) too.

As you get into the core reason of your debt problem, you would realize that you always have the power to deal with it. You need to stop blaming external circumstances right this moment.

Start taking back the power and stop blaming. Then only can you truly manage your debt and slowly eliminate debt in your life. I hope eliminating debt in your life is something important to you. If such, read on…

Chapter 3: The Detrimental Effects Of Being In Debt

I have grown to hate debt. Ever since I figured out how much interests I was paying on my credit cards each month and how it impacts my life, I took a conscious decision to get out of debt completely.

In the first chapter, I shared about the agony of being in debt. In this chapter, I would go deeper into the effects of being in debt. The purpose of this is to build your motivation to deal with debt better. As you read through this chapter, you would feel the 'pain' of being in debt. Make sure to fuel yourself with this motivation so you would be able to manage your debt better.

Unable To Enjoy Life

Debt is like putting myself into a jail cell. I hate debt. I know I have been saying quite a few times, but it is to reinforce the 'hatred' for debt in you too.

When you are in debt, your decisions are limited. You have no choice as to how to live your life. You have to stay in your dead-end job because you need to make ends meet. You can't try a new career that you are interested in. You can't go on a wonderful escapade if you want to. You are tied down.

Debt pulls you down and sucks the life out of you. You need to work in a job you hate and be with people you don't like simply to make the minimum monthly payments. Ever wonder why so many people complain about work? *Because they don't have a choice.*

The worst thing about debt as a single father looking to date again?

It makes it hard for me to meet women. I would be so busy making those monthly payments that my entire life is about work. You have no time to learn how to meet women, attract them and take them out on dates.

Unable To Be With Your Children

When you are in debt, you have less time to be with your children. For children, being with them is an indication that you love them. Children simply need your presence at home, especially when their parents have just been divorced.

With debt, you don't have the freedom for that. Even during meals, you are worried about work. You think that without that job, your life would be over. You wouldn't be able to pay the mortgage on the house and your children would be evacuated from the house.

Part of being a great single father is to have time for your children when they need you. Of course, it may be difficult for you to send them everywhere all the time, but you still need to have the freedom to spend the weekends with them. Do you have freedom to do so if you have debt?

Need To Work Longer Hours

Because you are trying to repay the debt, you have to work longer hours. Due to this longer working hours, your health takes a toll. You end up getting sick due to the stress of working long hours.

You would have to be admitted to hospital and your children would need to take care of you instead of the other way around.

Some single fathers I know of are constantly thinking about work that and nothing else. They work long hours trying to repay their debt and they don't have the presence of mind to be with their children.

Besides that, working longer hours also make you hate work. You hate the fact that you are always in your office and that your real 'home' is your office.

There are many people in this world who hate working in their jobs due to the insane hours but they simply have no choice because they need to make ends meet.

Stress All The Time

Being in debt is stressful. Your credit card company would constantly chase you to make payments. You are afraid to open up the letter that states how much you owe the credit card company. Worse still, you are afraid to check how much money you have in the bank.

You feel like someone is always behind your back, trying to get something from you. I hate the feeling when the bank would constantly chase me. Having debt is like 'working' for the bank.

Anger At Home

Stress at work means that you are angry at home too. You get affected easily by your children who are constantly bothering you. You feel that they are always creating problems when in fact, it is you who is stressed up.

You lash out at them whenever they do something that even slightly triggers you. You become agitated easily. Your children would hesitate from being close to you and the relationship you have with them only becomes worse.

* * *

From these reasons, make sure that you write down several reasons of your own too. Think about the ways your life would change when you wouldn't have debt.

Sit down and write the pain of having debt and the pleasure of NOT having debt. This would be your motivation to manage or eliminate your debt.

Chapter 4: Priority Expenses For A Single Father

From the previous chapter, it should be clear about the dangers of debt for a single father. I hope you come to a point where you hate debt as much as I do.

Ok. Probably it's a bit too much for me to expect you to hate debt, but I hope you get my point. Debt simply binds you to one spot and limits your choice in life.

Before we head into the more detailed methods of debt management, we would look into the various expenses that a single father would have. These expenses are a priority for a single father and would have to be managed well because they tend to be the expenses that would make or break your financial success as a single father.

- **Mortgage And Rent.** Housing is an important part for all single fathers. The key question is: Are you overpaying for it? Are you living in a house which is too big and the rental excessive? If you are, you would need to learn some strategies to manage your mortgage better.

- **Food.** Spending on food is something that you can't look to save much unless you have some skills (Resource: www.singledaddydating.com/couponing). This is a resource that many single fathers in my support group use to save money by couponing. It is an information product that ISN'T FREE, but extremely valuable.

You and your children need to eat. You want your children to grow up well. Using coupons can help you save a tremendous amount of money. However, there are other ways to save on food too if you are creative enough.

- **Utility Bills.** This is something you need to pay as long as you have a house. You would need to manage your consumption if you want to save money from your utility bills. For many homes in the United States, they are spending way too much on utility. Look for creative means to save money at home.

- **Alimony & Child Support.** These are mandatory after a divorce, if the court has ordered you to do so. What you need to do is to learn how to manage your ex-wife well. Besides that, it pays to have a good divorce lawyer deal with your divorce. You wouldn't want to pay excessive alimony. If you feel like you are paying too much, you can appeal for a modification

What are the priority expenses you have as a single father?

I didn't go in depth with the various expenses and how you can save money on them because this book isn't about helping you save money. Instead, this is simply for you to realize where you need to save in terms of trying to cut down spending and manage your debt better.

Take time to write down everything you spend in the past three months. Be as detailed as possible. If you can't do it, start today and record all the expenses you spend on for the next three months.

It may take you some time, but it would go a long way towards understanding where your money is going and making you a better financial planner.

Chapter 5: What Are You Entitled To?

As a single father, you should know that there is a way to deal with debt better. One of the ways is to simply make more first.

What? Make more first?

It doesn't have to be from your job.

Are you aware that you can get plenty of benefits, tax credits and maintenance from being a single father? Make sure that you maximize your 'income' when you utilise these benefits. Different states or countries have different legislations and you would need to check for them.

Your local advice agency would be able to do a 'benefits check' to ensure you are getting the most out of benefits. The following are the various financial help you can get as a single father:-

- **Income Support.** If you aren't available for full-time work in a case where you need to care for a young toddler and you don't have money to live on, you can apply for income support. How much you qualify and get would depend on your circumstances.

- **Employment And Support Allowance.** If you have an illness or disability that impacts your ability to work, this allowance would offer you personalised support and financial help.

- **Jobseekers' Allowance.** If you are in the process of finding for a new job, you can apply for this allowance.

- **Tax Credits.** These are considered payment from the government. If you are responsible for child/children, you can apply for these tax credits to make your life better.

- **Help With Housing.** Should you rent, you may be entitled to these housing benefits. You may pay all or part of your rent. Should you be paying a mortgage on your home, you would be entitled to some assistance on the interest payments of your mortgages.

- **Utility Bills.** If you have utility bills to pay, you can contact your utilities supplier and explain your situation. Unknown to many people, some utility companies allow you to pay off arrears in instalments and have deductions if you are a single parent.

Share with them your difficulties and see if you are qualified.

- **Social Fund.** Social funds are money allocated by the government to help people with low income. You would need to check if you are eligible for such social funds.

- **Help With Childcare And Education.** If you pay for childcare, you may be able to get tax credits. Depending on the place you are staying in, there are various benefits for children. Make sure to utilise them.

In truth, there are plenty of other support given to single fathers if they take the time to learn. Depending on where you are located, you would be able to find various benefits for single fathers to make your life easier.

These entitlements can help a single father a great deal in ensuring that he manages his spending better. Start now by checking your local municipal council to see what benefits you are entitled to.

Chapter 6: Eliminating Debt In Your Life

Take ten minutes to sit down in a quiet place. I want you to do some visualization. Imagine your life without debt.

Can you truly imagine yourself without any debt in life?

How would your life be? How are you freer or happier?

Life would be so 'light'. You live life everyday with no one bothering you about making those payments. Those unnecessary payment on the expensive car you bought, on the mindless credit card purchases and the high mortgage payments on your house. All these are totally gone.

Try to visualize a life without debt. As vivid as possible.

Many people struggle to imagine such a life. For them, debt has become a big part of their lives. They are used to living with debt in their lives that imagining a life without debt seems like they lack any purpose. It might be harsh for me to say this, but for some people, their 'purpose' in life is debt.

To eliminate debt requires a much disciplined approach. In Chapter 3 – The Detrimental Effects Of Being In Debt, I have shared about how you can create motivation from remembering the effects of having debt in life. Having the motivation gives you the drive to be disciplined in the process of eliminating debt.

From this chapter, you would learn a simple step-by-step guide towards eliminating debt. It has been used by many single fathers to eliminate debt in their lives effectively. The steps are:-

1. **Know Your Debt Number.** *What is your debt number? How much do you owe?* Take a piece of paper or open up a spreadsheet document on your computer. Write down all the debt that you have. Be thorough. Make sure you list every single debt that you have. Ensure you also include the exact number of how much you owe. Write down the interest charged on each item, if applicable.

2. **Have A Plan.** Develop a plan of repayment based on the income you have. Write down all the income you have. See how you can create a strategy to pay down the debt each month. Make it a priority by

creating a standing order at the beginning of each month. As your pay-check comes in each month, make it a point to automatically deduct it from your bank account. This automatic repayment trains you to use less money. Many people tend to spend on unnecessary items first before paying off their debt.

3. **Downsize Your Life.** This is perhaps the most important part of eliminating debt in your life. You need to focus on the areas of your life which are truly important to you. Then, you need to eliminate those expenses that aren't necessary. If you find yourself paying too much on mortgage each month, this may mean moving to a smaller house. Downsizing means focusing on the essentials in life. As you focus on the essentials, you have more money to pay off your debt. This gives you more freedom in the future.

4. **Put It In Writing.** The plan can't be done

in your mind because you tend to forget about it over time. Take time to list down your finances as thorough as possible. This includes:-

- How much you owe

- Your income

- How long it takes to pay off each debt

- Your 'downsize' list – What expenses are important and what you can eliminate

- Budget for every month

I have known single fathers who have kept journals to remind themselves of the money that they spend each month, together with their financial targets. This gives them a tracking tool to ensure that they are on track towards their financial goals.

5. Take Action. Eliminating debt is more than just about reducing expenses. It is also about increasing your income stream. You can look for methods to make more money. For many single fathers, the main factor that is preventing them from making more money is their lack of time. If that is a factor for you, you would also need to learn how to manage your time well. Managing your time well frees up your time to make more money.

* * *

Eliminating debt is something personal. These five steps are mere guidelines for single fathers who want to do something to improve their finances. For some people, they would want to make big changes and make drastic changes in their lifestyles.

I have known people who sold off their house and life in caravans for a few months to pay down the debt. It may sound very drastic, but it all boils down to how much you want to eliminate debt in your life.

If you are someone who wants is serious about eliminating debt, one great resource that can help you reduce the debt owing is National Debt Relief.

(http://www.singledaddydating.com/NDR)

This is an award-winning service that would easily help you with any long-term debt that you have. When you enroll in this proven debt consolidation program, you may be able to give less than you think. It helps to significantly reduce the amount of debt owing.

This resource is invaluable because you would be able to get a **FREE DEBT RELIEF QUOTE** and see how they would help you become debt free. You simply need to enter your details and they would come out with a solution for you.

Check it out...

http://www.singledaddydating.com/NDR)

Chapter 7: Financial Strategies For Single Fathers

It is not enough to simply eliminate debt. You need to think of a way to help you get ahead too. Eliminating debt and managing your expenses is playing the financial game on 'defense'. Playing 'defense' isn't sufficient for a single father to get ahead.

You would also need to play some 'offence' – that is making more money or having a plan towards financial success. These tips would help a single father get ahead in his financial life. They include:-

- **Create A Budgeting Plan.** You may reach a point in your life where you have no debt in your life. However, you still need to manage your finances. A budgeting plan help you to manage your spending. Again, this is about focusing on the essential spending you have in life. Following and sticking to a budget would help you make the most of the income that you bring in each month.

- **Set Aside For Emergencies.** Things happen unexpectedly. No one can predict what would happen in the future. You wouldn't want to get into debt should something unexpected happen in the future. Therefore, it is important for you to have an emergency fund. This emergency fund gives you the protection for both you and your children.

- **Let Your Children Help.** Do not try to

sugar-coat your financial situation to your children. If you are in financial difficulties, you have to communicate those problems to your children. You don't have to be very direct. You can let them know and see if they could help. This may mean including them in the budgeting process or letting them help in certain chores at home. You can even teach your children how to cook so that you can save money on eating out. They may also look to get a part time job to earn more money.

- **Childcare Is An Important Expense.** The cost of childcare can quickly become expensive. If you have children below the ages of twelve, childcare can be very important because it gives you more time and peace of mind. With this in place, you can have the peace of mind of making more money or handling other things that happen in your life better. Places like the YMCA have certain inexpensive school programs that can help you tremendously.

- **Flexible Working Hours.** See if your employer offers flexible working hours. See if you can do some work from home. This helps you avoid certain problems at work and ensures that you can care for your children if they are sick. With the extra time, you can even look to start your own stay-at-home business.

- **Plan For The Worst.** I hate to be pessimistic, but terrible things can happen sometimes. If you are the sole caregiver of your children, make sure that you have life insurance, a will or estate planning in place. Besides that, having guardianship documents also helps. This can be an even more important thing if your ex-spouse is a physical threat to you.

- **Take Care Of Yourself.** Even as single fathers, you need a little 'me time'. I take it all the time. It gives me the time to recharge and focus on myself. Don't feel guilty about spending some time for yourself. Doing this makes you a better parent. Give yourself a break by mingling with other people. One great group to mix with is by being around single parent support groups. You can share some notes about how to become a better parent and how to handle some situations better.

* * *

You would be surprised to know that many of these 'tips' aren't really financial advice. However, they are still important to your finances due to how it impacts your emotional well-being. The tips would greatly impact you and thus your financial health.

You can't afford to neglect your finances after you have no debt in your life. You still need to make a conscious effort to improve your financial life. Remember, it is about playing the financial game on 'offence' as well.

Chapter 8: Develop A Healthy Attitude Towards Debt

Debt is detrimental. Period.

Its convenience is a tip of a double-edged sword that most of society don't realize. It can help you if you know how to use it well, it will be detrimental to you if you don't. Personally, I believe that the number one killer in the world isn't cancer, stroke or heart attack.

The number one killer is debt.

Debt stresses up your life and because of it,

you develop these terminal illnesses.

If you aspire to life a debt-free lifestyle, that is very admirable. Living debt-free means you are free to live a joyful life without unnecessary commitments. It means that you are a happier person. Take time to check those countries with the most consumer debt, and you would find them to be among the unhappiest.

Think of debt as a jail sentence. It is you stepping into a prison cell voluntarily. Stupid? Yes it is!

If you have used the strategies in Chapter 6 – Eliminating Debt In Your Life to remove all the debt in your life, you still need to make sure that your life remains that way. You don't want to get back into the situation where you are still paying off debt in the future. You want to develop great financial habits that make sure you won't fall back into debt.

Living a debt-free lifestyle would make you happier and freer. You become a better father and enjoy life much more.

If you have yet to completely eliminate debt from your life, look to manage it better. Make sure that you are slowly reducing the debt you have and that you don't add more debt in to your life.

You can start to take a basic course in personal finance. Such courses have tremendous benefits. They allow you to know how to draw up a basic expenses plan and know where you are heading financially.

It also teaches you the basics of budgeting and plan your process to eliminate debt and build wealth. Even if you already eliminate all debt in your life, it helps to attend these courses.

For some people, their debt may be so huge that they simply can't see themselves eliminating their debt in the short term. If you can't see yourself eliminating debt in 12 months, look to make it longer term. See if you can eliminate it within 5 years or so.

The most important thing in this situation is to focus. You need to focus on the goal ahead. Take steps to ensure that you are making a move, however slow you are. Develop the right attitude towards money and debt. You would find yourself in a position where you are free sooner than you imagine.

Most importantly, don't increase the amount of debt you owe. It can be tempting to buy the latest electronic gadget or clothing, but think of those purchases like a prison sentence, putting you in a jail. You are only digging yourself a deeper hole.

Chapter 9: Develop An Attitude Of Prosperity

I have mentioned many times about the importance of thinking beyond debt.

Such thinking is important because you want to get ahead as a single father. You need to think of your children's future needs like college, in case of emergency and even for your retirement fund.

If you are to provide for all of these, it is crucial for you to develop an attitude of prosperity. This is also the attitude of abundance.

What Is An Abundant Attitude

Do you think this world is abundant or scarce?

This one questions determines how you look at life. If you treat life as abundant, your mindset is different. If you treat life as scarce, your mindset different.

Having an abundant mindset means thinking that there are tons of opportunities in life. The money you have isn't limited. You can make tons of money in life. Don't think of it as something where it doesn't 'grow on trees'. There are plenty of opportunities out there and you only need to take advantage of it.

Start to see life as a place where there are endless opportunities to make more money. It is a place where debt doesn't exist and something which is created in your mind. You have tons of ways to make great money.

Despite the portrayal of the world as a scarce and limited place by the media, it is not such. Opportunities are created in a heartbeat. New technology creates endless opportunities. It is only up to you to take them.

For now, it can be hard for you to believe it because you have been trained into an attitude of scarcity. You have been brought up to believe that this world is a limiting place by your parents and teachers. But, give it some time.

Take time to visualize a world of abundance. Start to see yourself having so many wonderful things in life. Feel the gratitude for living in an abundant world and the tons of wonderful things you can experience.

As you start to develop this mindset, you find that ways of making more money would appear in your life. It gives you an avenue to build more wealth into your life.

Stop thinking so much about the debt that you have in life. Thinking about debt only makes you feel that this world is scarce. It would only perpetuate a 'debt-mentality'.

Change your mentality from one which is constantly fighting against debt to one where you are looking to build wealth.

Over time, this wealth-building mindset becomes an integral part of yourself. You feel empowered to live life on the 'offence' and money making opportunities present themselves to you easily.

However, it is also important for you to have a good savings nest for this journey to abundance. This savings serve as an emergency and is also important for your children. Saving constantly allows you to take more risks in your life. This may include starting a new business or trying a new career path.

By saving, you can also do a lot of good for your children. You teach them the value of saving money for a rainy day.

Final Notes

Debt management is more of an emotional thing rather than a strategic thing. Many single fathers, when looking to manage their debt, focus on the strategy required for debt management (or elimination).

Although the strategy to manage debt is important, without having a proper emotional blueprint towards debt, it can be difficult for single fathers to execute. Knowing the strategy without having the right emotional fortitude only makes them go in rounds. They know what to do, but they simply can't find the motivation to do it.

It is like healthy eating. We know the importance of eating healthy and eliminating fast food in our daily lives. However, we still eat unhealthily. Why? Because we don't have the emotional fortitude to do it. We don't have enough drive to do it.

Some single father may have debt problems and look for strategies to manage it. Some learn those methods religiously but still find it hard to execute them. That is when they have a motivation problem.

They may constantly say that they want to eliminate debt and know of all the strategies needed, but without this emotional drive, it is useless.

Therefore, you need to develop this 'hunger' to eliminate debt in your life. Reread Chapter 3 – The Detrimental Effects Of Being In Debt. Make sure that you internalize the pain that comes when you have debt in your life. Read until you feel the pain.

Remember the pain of not being with your children. The pain of having to work in a job that you have no passion. The pain of missing your children's recitals because of a crazy long-hours job…

And the many other pains of being in debt.

That should be good enough motivation. I wish you luck in your debt elimination process.

LEAVE A REVIEW

I hope this book has helped you well. It isn't my intention at all to go deep into the topic. I am no expert in everything. However, I have the help of many other single fathers who have shared with me their invaluable experience.

If this book has helped you in any way, do leave me a review. This helps build our single father community.

If you feel that this book can be improved in any way, do mention it in the review. I would love to hear from you.

I wish you luck as a single father…

ABOUT NICK THOMAS

Nicholas Thomas has helped many single fathers cope with divorce in the past few years. By helping them gain more confidence and stability in their lives, he is able to guide them towards being a man that attracts other women easily.

He divorced back in 2008 and knows how difficult a divorce can be for a man. It was a terrible time for him when he got his divorce. He envisioned his children blaming him and not being able to spend time with him. It gave him a constant guilt trip.

Being a divorced man can be very difficult. Ever since his 'emotional recovery' from the divorce, he has helped many single fathers by advising and helping them gain confidence.

Should you want to share your story with him, you can do so at
www.singledaddydating.com/shareastory/

DEBT MANAGEMENT

ALSO BY NICK THOMAS

(1) Dating After Divorce For The Single Daddy

(2) Dating Ideas For The Single Daddy

(3) How To Be An Alpha Male

(4) First Date Conversations

(5) Online Dating

(6) How To Approach Women

(7) Mature Dating

(8) Single Parent Support

(9) Coping With Divorce

(10) Parenting After Divorce

Visit www.singledaddydating.com/bookstore/

NICK THOMAS		www.singledaddydating.com

Get Your Complimentary
FREE BOOK

Join our community today and get **10 Crucial Checklist To Dating Success For Single Fathers** FREE, delivered right to your email…

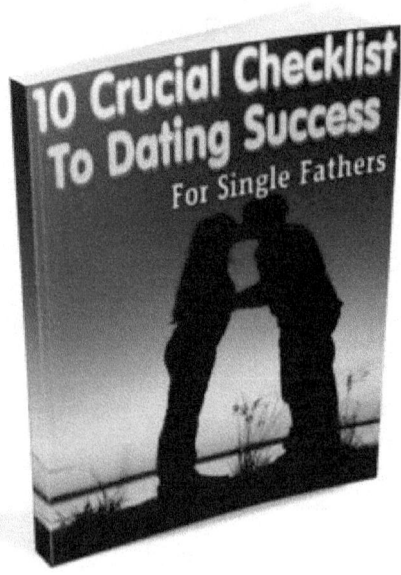

JOIN US AT
WWW.SINGLEDADDYDATING.COM/ NEWSLETTER/

www.ingramcontent.com/pod-product-compliance
Lightning Source LLC
Chambersburg PA
CBHW071810170526
45167CB00003B/1246